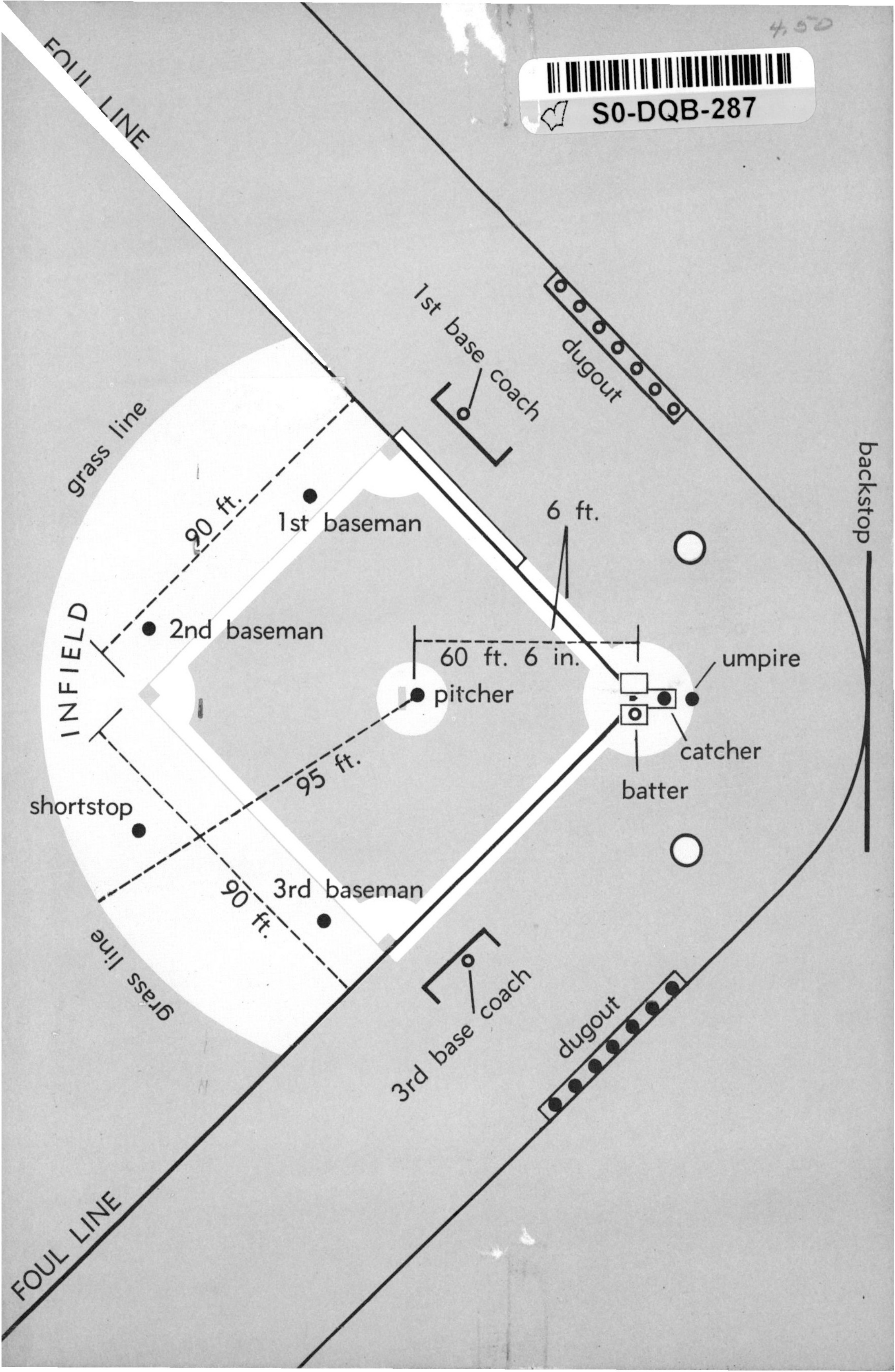

FOUL LINE

grass line

1st base coach

dugout

backstop

6 ft.

90 ft.

1st baseman

2nd baseman

INFIELD

60 ft. 6 in.

pitcher

umpire

95 ft.

batter

catcher

shortstop

3rd baseman

90 ft.

grass line

3rd base coach

dugout

FOUL LINE

WORLD SERIES HIGHLIGHTS

FOUR FAMOUS CONTESTS

BY GUERNSEY VAN RIPER, JR.

GARRARD PUBLISHING COMPANY
CHAMPAIGN, ILLINOIS

Sports Consultant:
COLONEL RED REEDER
Former Member of the West Point Coaching Staff
and
Former Special Assistant to the West Point
Director of Athletics

Photo credits:

Brown Brothers: pp. 56, 61, 71, 72, 77, 79, 84, 87, 90
Culver Pictures: pp. 64, 80 (both)
MacGreevy Collection, Boston Public Library: pp. 6–7, 9
United Press International, Inc.: pp. 1, 3, 4, 16, 23, 27, 30 (both), 33, 36, 37, 39, 45, 55, 62–63, 68, 91, jacket
Wide World Photos: pp. 12 (both), 19, 22, 25, 42, 48, 51, 53, 94

Contents

Safe at second! Doby's slide for Cleveland
captures the thrill of World Series play.

1 How It All Began

Baseball champions of the world!

Every year there's a battle for this title. Millions of people get excited about it, whether they are baseball fans or not. The *real* baseball enthusiasts can't think of anything else during those days when the American League champion takes the field against the National League champion.

Every October, for more than 60 years, these two big professional leagues have sent their winning teams into a "World

Series." Why is it a "world" series? We believe that no other country plays our national game as well as we do, so the champion of the United States is considered world champion as well.

The National League has been playing baseball since 1876. By 1900 it had established itself as the best league, playing the

In 1894 the Orioles and Giants fought for the National League championship.

most expert baseball. Many cities wanted to have teams in the National League, but by 1900 it had settled down to eight teams. Players in the minor leagues and on other teams around the country all hoped for a chance to be called up to one of the "big league" teams.

The National League drew up a schedule of games every year, so that every team played a number of games with every other team in all the different cities of the league: New York, Boston, Philadelphia, Chicago, Pittsburgh, St. Louis, Brooklyn, and Cincinnati. At the end of the season the team with the best percentage of victories became National League champion. The rivalry among the teams and the fans in their home cities was intense.

Since so many cities were clamoring for a chance to have "big league" baseball, the Western League was expanded to become the American League in 1901. Chiefly through the efforts of one man, Ban Johnson, soon they, too, had an eight-team league. They grabbed players from everywhere—from the National League when they could—and they moved into several National League cities with opposing teams.

"Those upstarts will never last. They're not even worth considering," scoffed the National League managers.

But the American League rolled merrily on, playing a full schedule of games and drawing large crowds. In 1903 the Boston team won the American League flag and promptly challenged Pittsburgh, National

Pittsburgh at Boston, October 3, 1903, the first game of the modern World Series

League winner, to a post-season series. The confident Boston Red Sox beat the Pittsburgh Pirates and became the "world" champion for that year.

The next year the New York Giants were the National League champions. They refused to play in a post-season series. "They've stolen our players and tried to wreck our league," the National League's Giants complained about the American Leaguers. But there was such a howl from the fans and the newspaper reporters that the two leagues agreed to make peace and become friendly rivals. They drew up rules for a yearly series to begin in 1905, and they have played every year since.

In the last twenty years a new wave of interest has changed the big leagues a lot. Teams have moved out of their original home cities. New cities have fought for the right to have a major league baseball club.

By 1969 there were twelve teams in the National League and twelve teams in the American League representing every section of the country. And even more teams are to be added. 1969 also brought a new play-off system to determine league winners.

Such increased interest and competition only add to the excitement of the post-season battle for the title of world champion. The series has come to be called our "annual fall classic"—one of the greatest events on the American sports calendar.

You will read about four of the most brilliant battles for the world title in this book, from the present right back to the "good old days" of that first series. No more exciting World Series games have ever been played than the 1968 series that opens our story.

Denny McLain

Bob Gibson

2 The Tigers Refuse to be Beaten

"What a battle that will be: Gibson vs. McLain!"

Long before the 1968 baseball season was over, fans were talking about the great pitching duel they expected to see in the World Series.

In the National League race, the world champion St. Louis Cardinals jumped into the lead, and stayed there. Helping to mow down the opposition for the Cards was their great pitcher, Bob Gibson. Thirteen times he shut out the opposing team. Already the tall, gangling speedballer had starred in two World Series. In 1964 he pitched and won his last two full games for the Cards; in 1967 he boosted his record to five straight by winning three more complete games to help the Cards to their eighth world championship.

In the American League a new star pitcher was setting records as he led the Detroit Tigers toward their first championship in 23 years. A chunky, black-haired hero named Denny McLain piled up the most victories for the power-hitting Tigers. Thirty-one times McLain crushed the opposition—the first time in 37 years a major league pitcher had won that many games. Naturally, McLain was a great favorite with the Detroit fans. The talkative Denny was also a talented jazz organist.

Busch Stadium in St. Louis was packed to the limit, with more than 50,000 fans, when the Cardinals and the Tigers met on Wednesday, October 2, for the first game of the 1968 series. The happy, excited crowd gave a big cheer for both teams as they warmed up. Millions tuned in to watch on television. The Tiger team snapped the ball around in a fast pre-game drill; then the Cards took over, their red and white uniforms flashing in the sun as they took their last practice throws. It was going to be more than a battle between two pitchers; two powerful teams were ready to fight for baseball's biggest prize.

Sports writers were predicting that the Tigers could never stop the fast, aggressive Cardinals.

"The Cardinals will take the Series in five games," claimed some of the experts. Big Bob Gibson started out to prove them right. The tall, lanky 32-year-old pitcher from Omaha was in top form as he pitched to the eager Tigers. His long legs flying as he made his delivery, he got every ounce of power into each pitch. His long right arm whipped the ball toward the plate with tremendous speed.

The Tigers were expecting his great speed, but Gibson surprised them with his

This composite photo shows pitcher Bob Gibson in action on the mound.

sharp-breaking curve. Down went the Tiger batters, one after another. They missed the ball, or they failed to connect solidly. Gibson was blowing them right out of the park.

For three innings Denny McLain held off the Cardinals, too. He worked more slowly, taking his time on each pitch, bouncing the ball in his glove, adjusting his cap. But in the fourth inning, Denny lost his touch. The man who had seldom given bases on balls throughout the season walked two Cardinals on eight straight pitches. The next two batters hit singles, and suddenly the Cards led, 3-0.

Bob Gibson didn't need anything more. The sweat glistened on his forehead as he fired away; he continued his mastery over the Tigers. One by one the strikeouts mounted up. The Cardinals increased their lead to 4-0 in the seventh inning, when jack-rabbit Lou Brock connected for a Cardinal home run.

When the ninth inning opened, Gibson had struck out 14 Tigers. The first batter got a single, only the fifth hit for the Tigers. With three strong hitters coming up, the fans stirred in expectation. But Gibson was equal to the task. One after the other he struck them all out. The first one was number 15, tying the World Series record for strikeouts. Then as the next two Tigers went down on strikes, the fans set up a steady roar. The scoreboard proclaimed new records: first 16, then 17 strikeouts as the mighty Gibson won a shutout victory.

The Cards were off to a brilliant start. What could the Tigers do the next day to halt their drive?

"The Tigers' next best pitcher is lefty Mickey Lolich," the newspapers reported, "and the Cardinals have been eating up left-handers all year long."

Nevertheless Mickey was there, and the Cards found him a hard nut to crack. Solidly built, with a smooth, compact throwing motion, Mickey was surprisingly fast. And he had a quick curve that caught the Cards napping time after time.

What's more, Tiger power hitters finally

Willie Horton has just made the spectacular second-inning hit that will bring him home.

cut loose. In the second inning the Tigers went ahead on Willie Horton's smash into the bleachers for a home run. The husky outfielder had a grin a mile wide as he crossed home plate.

Mickey Lolich came to bat in the next inning. He took a swing at a high fast ball. No one was more astounded than Mickey when the ball soared far and free into the stands for a home run, the first one he had ever hit in the big leagues.

Tigers bats rang out again for three runs in the sixth. They led, 5–0. Then the Cards threatened in the last of the inning. Up came Lou Brock, a terror on the base paths to National League teams all year long. Lou got a walk—and promptly stole second. A couple of hits brought him home, but the Tigers choked off the rally with a quick double play.

Next the Tigers pushed over three more

runs to increase their lead. Fighting back, the dangerous Lou Brock singled and stole another base for the Cards, but the team couldn't score. The game ended: Tigers, 8; Cardinals, 1.

The series was tied at one game apiece. With a day off for travel, the teams moved to Tiger Stadium in Detroit for the next three games.

Now the Tigers were playing before their own hometown fans, and they moved ahead early in Saturday's game. With a man on base in the third inning, Detroit's 16-year veteran, Al Kaline came to the plate. Though he was the best hitter the Tigers had in many years, Kaline had never had a chance to play in a World Series before.

Kaline hit a mighty wallop into the stands, and Detroit led, 2-0.

But in the fifth the Cardinals turned on their speed and power. Pesky Lou Brock started it with another hit. He danced off first base and stole second—for the third time in the game. He was enough to shake up any team. This time centerfielder Curt Flood drove him home. A walk put another Card on base, and the next hitter, Cepeda, hit a popfly. Then McCarver slammed a home run into the upper deck in right.

In the third game, Lou Brock steals second base, below, and Tim McCarver crosses the plate with a three-run homer, right.

Three more runs scored and the Cards led, 4-2.

They were ahead to stay. Another three-run homer in the seventh put the game out of reach. The score was Cardinals, 7; Tigers, 3.

Sunday's game brought another great crowd to Tiger stadium. In spite of rain that delayed the start of the game for half an hour, there wasn't an empty seat. Tiger fans had high hopes that Denny McLain would make a strong comeback against Bob Gibson.

Tiger hopes were jolted when the first Cardinal came up to bat. The ever-dangerous Lou Brock connected with one of McLain's high fast balls for a home run. Before the inning was over another run crossed the plate and the Cards led, 2-0.

Big Bob Gibson strode to the mound for the Cards. Once again he was pitching in top form and the Tiger hitters couldn't break through.

As the third opened, the Cards struck again with three solid hits that brought two more runs. Then the skies opened up and rain fell for more than an hour. Grounds keepers rushed out to unroll a tarpaulin to protect the infield.

There was a buzz of excitement from the fans and the players and the umpires.

The rain over, ground crews at Tiger Stadium remove the tarpaulin and the game goes on.

Could the game continue? Or would it be called off and the Cards lose their four runs? Would Gibson cool off and lose his effectiveness with such a long wait?

Finally the rain stopped and the umpires shouted, "Play ball!" Gibson set down the Tigers again.

It was McLain who failed to return. His shoulder was so sore he couldn't pitch.

But the Cards continued their rampage. Bob Gibson turned slugger by knocking out a home run to open the fourth. Lou Brock tripled and came home on an infield out.

With the score 6-0 the Tigers' Jim Northrup got hold of a Gibson pitch for a home run. Sadly for the Tigers, that was all. The Cards poured over four more in the eighth, with Lou Brock accounting for the last three with a booming triple.

The Cards won, 10-1. It was a new

St. Louis fans applauded Bob Gibson, left,
and Lou Brock, right, heroes of the game.

record for Gibson, with his seventh straight
World Series win. Lou Brock stole his
seventh base, tying his own World Series
record. And Lou's hitting percentage shot
him ahead of all past performers for total
World Series games played.

The newspapers acclaimed: "COLLAPSE
OF TIGERS APPEARS COMPLETE." With

a 3-1 lead in games, the Cards needed just one more game to win a second-straight world championship. The next day they went after it with another barrage of hitting.

The Tigers had Mickey Lolich, their only winning pitcher, on the mound. On the first pitch he faced the most brilliant Cardinal of them all, Lou Brock. Lou connected for a ringing double. Curt Flood singled. The next Cardinal whacked a home run, and the score was Cards, 3; Tigers, 0.

Out to the mound went the Detroit manager to talk things over with Lolich. Very calmly he cautioned Mickey not to press too hard, to stick to his regular smooth pitching motion. Mickey insisted he was all right now; he just hadn't had enough time to warm up before the game.

Lolich proceeded to stop the Cards. At

last in the fourth the Tiger bats rang with two triples and a single. Now it was Cards, 3; Tigers, 2.

Once again in the fifth the rampaging Lou Brock cut loose with a long double. When the next Card hit a short single to left, Lou dashed for home. In left field the Tigers' Willie Horton grabbed the ball on one bounce and fired it home with all the power he could muster. Straight and true it went to the Tiger catcher just in time to tag out Lou Brock before he crossed the plate.

Tiger fans went wild. They felt that the tide was turning in their favor. They kept up their uproar as Mickey Lolich worked his way out of one jam after the other.

In the top of the seventh Lolich started a Tiger rally by dumping a short pop-fly into right field for a safe hit. The next

Pitcher Mickey Lolich,
left, goes into action;
Al Kaline, below, hits
one into center field in
the seventh.

Tiger hit safely. Then came a walk, and the bases were full of Tigers ready to head for home.

Veteran Al Kaline was next. After sixteen years of waiting, here was his biggest chance. He swung sharply and lined a solid base hit to center field. Two runs crossed the plate and the Tigers went out in front, 4-3. The next Tiger got a hit, too, and another run came in.

Now it was up to Lolich to hold the lead. He put the Cards down with no more runs. The last man to face him was Lou Brock. This time all Lou could do was hit a short tap that Lolich grabbed and threw to first.

With a 5-3 victory, the Tigers refused to be counted out.

Now the scene shifted back to Busch Stadium in St. Louis for the windup of the series. With a day of rest, and back in their own park, the Cards were confident they would get the decisive fourth victory.

It was a big surprise when Denny McLain went out to pitch the next game for the Tigers. But Denny had taken treatments for his sore shoulder, and he insisted that he was ready. After losing twice to the Cards, Denny was determined to show why he was the American League's leading pitcher.

In the second inning the Tigers staked Denny to a 2-0 lead. But that was only a warm-up. In the third the Tiger bats really boomed. For 37 minutes the Tigers bombarded four Cardinal pitchers. Al Kaline hit two singles. Jim Northrup hit a home run with the bases full. The Tigers put across 10 runs, the biggest World Series inning in 39 years. Only the Philadelphia Athletics had done it before—in 1929.

Denny McLain breezed along, just as he had all year. With the aches in his shoulder eased, he held the Cards scoreless until he yielded a single run in the ninth.

The amazing Tigers had smashed out a 13-1 victory to tie the series at three games apiece. Now everything hinged on

Ailing Denny McLain gave up only one run to the Cards despite a sore shoulder.

Thursday's game at Busch Stadium. The Cards were ready with their great pitcher, Bob Gibson, who had set down the Tigers twice. And who could go to the mound for the Tigers? It had to be Mickey Lolich who had surprised everyone by winning two games, too.

There wasn't one vacant seat in the stadium when the game opened. Gibson got huge applause when he took the mound. His powerful delivery looked as commanding as ever. His fast ball over-powered the Tiger batters. His control was perfect as he put the ball just where he wanted it. The first ten Tigers to face him went down in order as the fans cheered every pitch. In the fourth the Tigers got a man on base with a scratch hit. Gibson just pitched harder. He set down the *next* ten Tigers in order.

But the Cards could not break through Mickey Lolich. They figured they could wear him down, for Mickey was pitching with only two days' rest. Instead, Mickey's smooth delivery continued to baffle the Cards' eager hitters. When he began to tire and lose his speed, he used his sinker ball to keep the Cards off balance.

In the sixth, the brilliant Lou Brock smashed out a single. He danced off first, daring Lolich to catch him. Mickey watched him carefully. Suddenly he threw to first. Brock headed for second with amazing speed. But a quick throw from the Tiger first baseman nailed the Cards' big troublemaker at second. Tiger fans roared with relief, and the huge crowd of Cardinal rooters groaned. Speedy Curt Flood beat out an infield hit. He, too, danced off first to rattle the Tiger pitcher. But Mickey Lolich was ready again. A

He's out! Lou Brock is tagged at second.

quick throw caught Flood leading off first, and he was run down between bases. The great threat from the Cards' "speed boys" was snuffed out.

In the last of the seventh the Tigers broke through Gibson. Two batters went out, but the next two bounced singles through the infield. Then up came Jim Northrup, who had hit the bases-loaded home run the day before.

Gibson fired a steaming low pitch.

Northrup was ready. He drove the ball on a line toward deep center. Curt Flood, the best centerfielder in the major leagues, started forward, then turned back as he saw how hard the ball was hit. There was a gasp from the crowd as Flood lost his footing. He ran back as fast as he could, but Northrup's drive sailed over his head for a triple. Two Tiger runs crossed the plate. A minute later Northrup crossed

A mighty swing by Tiger Jim Northrup results in a grand-slam homer in the third inning.

the plate on another Tiger single. All of a sudden the Tigers were three runs up.

Now it was up to Lolich. Could he continue to hold the fighting Cards? Pitching carefully, he set them down in the seventh and eighth. In the ninth, his Tiger mates added a run to their lead; three singles off Gibson made the score 4-0.

Lolich pitched carefully in the last half inning. He got the first two batters out. Then Card third baseman Mike Shannon laced one into the left-field seats for a home run. The Cards fans jumped to their feet, yelling for more. But the next Card batter lifted a foul near the Cards' dugout. The Tiger catcher threw off his mask, raced back, and caught it for the last out. Then he grabbed Mickey Lolich with a great shout and a bear hug. In an instant all the Tigers surrounded their sturdy left-hander.

Shouting with joy, Mickey Lolich is carried off the field by catcher Bill Freehan.

The Tigers had won the final game, 4-1. They had won the World Series with an amazing comeback, a rally worthy of real champions. Mickey Lolich, the "second-best" pitcher, had come into his own as the biggest hero of the series.

"We thought we could hit him," groaned the Cards, "but he was just too good; he never let down."

3 The Big "B's" Beat Boston

The city of Boston was "baseball mad" in the fall of 1948. Both the Boston Braves and the Boston Red Sox were battling to the top in their leagues. It looked as though there might be an all-Boston World Series.

In the National League the Boston Braves pulled away to victory ahead of the St. Louis Cardinals by a comfortable margin. Braves fans celebrated their first pennant in 34 years. In the American League, the Boston Red Sox came up with a last-day-of-the-season victory and went into a tie for the championship. For the first time in history the American League had to order a playoff game for the pennant. Just one more victory, and it would be Boston Braves vs. Boston Red Sox for the world championship.

But then the Cleveland Indians came to town.

In the all-important playoff game the Boston Red Sox were wrecked, 8-3, by Cleveland's big "B" boys: Lou Boudreau and Gene Bearden. So it was Cleveland's turn to celebrate its first pennant in 28 years—and to get ready for the Boston Braves in the World Series.

Winning the pennant was a great triumph for Cleveland's handsome Lou Boudreau. Lou was a rarity in baseball: he played shortstop and managed the team, too. What's more, he was the

Cleveland's manager-shortstop, Lou Boudreau, in action in a late-season game in 1948.

youngest man ever to be named manager of a major league team when, aged twenty-four, he was chosen to lead the Indians. Still called the "Boy Manager," he brought his team through to the pennant after seven tough years.

Lou's brilliant play at shortstop led the Indians to triumph in the big playoff game. He made the miraculous pickups and sensational acrobatic plays for which he was famous, in spite of weak ankles that were always heavily taped. And he slammed out two home runs and two singles to lead the Indians' attack.

As his playoff pitcher, Boudreau used the popular freshman Gene Bearden, wounded navy hero. After a shaky start, Bearden settled down and stopped the Red Sox sluggers. Mixing his steaming fast ball and his tantalizing knuckle ball, he kept the Boston hitters off balance.

Bearden's victory topped off a great year for him. He was lucky to be in baseball at all. His ship had been sunk in World War II, and Gene had spent months in hospitals recovering. Patched up, with metal plates in his head and leg, he went out to show he was as good as anyone.

Now with the American League pennant under their belts, could the Cleveland Indians keep up their pace against the National League Boston Braves?

"No!" was the answer of thousands of Boston fans packed into Braves Field two days later. For a while it looked as though they were right. The Indians and the Braves collided in one of the great pitchers' duels of World Series history.

To the mound for the Indians, Boudreau sent his famous speed-ball pitcher and strike-out king, Bobby Feller. Now, after ten seasons of baffling American League

Johnny Sain, Boston's star pitcher, held the Cleveland team score-less in the first game of the 1948 Series.

batters and four years away for Navy service, Feller was itching for his first chance at a World Series game.

Pitching for the Boston Braves was the National League's best, right-hander Johnny Sain. Since returning from war service, hefty Johnny had been a big winner for the Braves.

For seven full innings the determined pitchers battled, each one in top form. On both sides, most of the batters hit harmless flies or struck out. On the scoreboard there were only "goose eggs."

Then came the eighth. Feller pitched carefully to the first Braves hitter, but he gave him a base on balls. Quickly the runner moved to second when the next Brave laid down a sacrifice bunt.

Feller bounced the ball in his glove as he faced the next batter. The runner on second took a big lead off base, ready to head for home, as the fans roared. Feller looked back at the runner, then toward the plate. The catcher flashed a secret signal to him and to Lou Boudreau at shortstop.

Feller prepared to pitch. Instead he suddenly whirled and threw toward second. Boudreau raced in, caught the throw, and tagged the runner sliding frantically back.

It looked as though the runner were out. But the umpire shouted "safe!"

Boudreau protested loudly, "I got him! I got him!" The Braves fans howled in relief. The Braves runner planted himself on the base while the argument went on. Finally the umpire walked away, with Lou still arguing and waving his arms.

The next Braves hitter flied out. Tommy Holmes then slammed a ground single past second base and the Braves runner raced home safely. It was the only score of the game. Sain got the Indians out in the ninth. He had won the tightest World Series game in 25 years and bested the great Bob Feller. Braves, 1; Indians, 0.

Next day Boudreau and his boys came back fighting. Lou had his pitcher ready: strong-armed Bob Lemon. After the war Lou had persuaded Bob to give up the outfield and become a pitcher. Bob Lemon responded by developing into one of the American League's best.

The Braves went after Lemon in the first inning and pushed one run across. But Lemon snuffed out the rally by catching a runner off second on the same play that failed for Feller. From then on Lemon baffled the Braves with his pet "sinker" pitch. They didn't get another run.

Boudreau (No. 5) takes a throw from Bob Lemon and tags out a Boston runner at second.

Boudreau started a two-run rally for the Indians with a double in the fourth, then he drove out the Braves pitcher with a single in the fifth. The Indians went on to win by 4–1 and tie the series.

It was a scramble for both teams to get on the train for Cleveland to play the next day. Then they barely had time to reach the huge Municipal Stadium in time for the game. In spite of rain, over 70,000 ardent Indians fans showed up to shout for a victory. And Gene Bearden gave the fans plenty to shout about.

In the strong breezes blowing off Lake Erie, Bearden's knuckle ball danced and floated before the anxious Braves batters. The Indians rooters howled in glee as Bearden set down the enemy scoreless, inning after inning.

Bearden turned batting hero, too, in the

third, when he drove a long double and went on to score the Indians' first run. He added a single in the next inning as the Indians scored their second and final run. Indians, 2; Braves, 0.

Next day Cleveland was a wild city. More than 81,000 fans packed the stadium, a new World Series record. The Boston Braves were keyed up to fight back, with their ace Johnny Sain ready to take the mound again. Crafty Johnny pitched another good game, but it was not quite good enough.

Lou Boudreau drove home a Cleveland run in the first inning with a long two-base hit. Then in the third another Cleveland hero stepped forward, young Larry Doby, the first Negro to play in the American League. With one smashing blow the speedy outfielder gave the Indians their margin of victory. He hit the first

Larry Doby crosses home plate after hitting the first home run of the 1948 Series.

home run of the series into deep right center field. So the Indians won again, 2–1. Now only one more victory was needed.

"Bob Feller will do it!" was the cry on Sunday. Into the lakefront stadium surged the largest crowd that had ever attended a baseball game—86,288 persons. They were sure Feller would win and this would be the last game of the series.

Up to now every game had been a pitchers' battle. Suddenly the hitters took over. In the very first inning the fighting Braves from Boston knocked in three runs off Bobby Feller. The Cleveland Indians fought back and, at the end of six innings, the score was tied at 5–5.

Then the game became a nightmare for the Indians. In the seventh the Braves cut loose again. They hit, they walked, they ran, they refused to be put out.

Poor Bobby Feller couldn't stop them. He trudged sadly back to the bench. This day he just didn't have the stuff. Three more Indians pitchers tried it, one after the other. When the Braves finally were out, six crushing runs had crossed the plate. Final score: Braves, 11; Indians, 5.

So it was back to Boston for Monday's game. Braves Field rocked with 40,000 fans eager to see the Braves tie the series. But for seven innings big Bob Lemon held the Braves at bay. For the Indians, Lou Boudreau rifled a double to bring in the first run. When the eighth opened, the Indians had built up a 4–1 lead.

And then, suddenly, the Braves filled the bases.

Cleveland's Bob Lemon on the mound, pitching against Detroit

"Come on, boys, show us how you make six runs!" pleaded the Braves rooters.

"Lemon's lost his stuff!" they shouted in glee.

For once, Lou Boudreau could agree with the Braves fans. So he sent in Gene Bearden to pitch in Lemon's place. It wasn't easy to stop the fired-up Braves. One run came across on a sacrifice fly. A long double brought in another run, a double that was almost a home run.

Then Bearden grabbed a ground ball off the bat of the next Braves hitter and threw him out to end the inning.

With the score Indians, 4; Braves, 3, Bearden stopped the Braves in the ninth. The game was over, the series was over, and the Cleveland Indians became world champions. On two Mondays in a row, Bearden had smashed the hopes of two Boston teams.

The jubilant Indians lift Gene Bearden to their shoulders after their brilliant win.

Lou Boudreau dashed over from short-stop and grabbed Bearden around the neck.

"I knew you'd do it, Gene," he shouted.

And the rest of the happy Cleveland Indians surrounded the two big "B's" who had battered the Boston Braves.

Note: The Boston team moved to Milwaukee in 1953, and then in 1966 to Georgia, to become the Atlanta Braves.

4 The Terrible Twins

Baseball was a swinging game in 1928. Both leagues had switched from the "dead" ball to the new "lively" ball. Batters were swinging harder, and aiming at the fences. Fans loved to see that home-run ball sail into the bleachers. And the champion home-run hitter of them all performed for the New York Yankees—the mighty Babe Ruth. In the 1927 season he set the record by belting out 60 home runs. In spite of a batting slump, a painfully sore muscle, and a weak ankle, he knocked

"The mighty Babe Ruth"

out 54 in 1928, bringing his team the league championship. But just before the World Series, he twisted his knee. And that was just the beginning of bad luck for the Yankees.

"LOU GEHRIG KNOCKED OUT," the newspaper headlines read a few days later, just after the last game of the season. "ANOTHER KEY PLAYER HURT AS WORLD CHAMPION NEW YORK YAN-KEES CLINCH THE PENNANT."

Big, hard-working Lou Gehrig had been hit full in the face by a batted ball. The injuries to the Yankee first baseman were painful but not serious. Through hugely swollen lips he told reporters, "I'll be ready for the World Series."

Star pitcher Herb Pennock was out of the series with a sore arm. The other Yankee pitchers were tired after a tough fight for the pennant with Connie Mack's

Athletics. Earle Combs, fleet outfielder, was out, too, with a badly broken finger.

Joe Dugan would play third, with a bad knee; Mark Koenig short, with a bruised heel; and Tony Lazzerri second, with an arm so sore he could hardly lift it. A line-up with six key players ailing was a bad way to start the series.

No wonder most of the sportswriters predicted the Yankees would lose to the National League winner, the St. Louis Cardinals. Hadn't the Cardinals beaten the Yanks two years before? Hadn't their pitchers stopped that "Murderers' Row" of Yankee sluggers—even those "Terrible Twins," Ruth and Gehrig?

"If the Yanks could play like last year, when they walloped Pittsburgh four straight times, they'd have a chance," said one sportswriter. "But how can they, with all their injuries?"

In the Yankee dressing room, Babe Ruth disagreed. The trainer for the New York team was working on his knee with heat and liniment. The big fellow growled, "Aw, how do they get that way, calling us easy meat? We'll bump them off, and I don't mean maybe!"

Sixty-thousand fans came out to Yankee Stadium on October 4 to see what would happen. The series was now being broadcast by radio all over the country. Millions waited to listen. In stores and offices in New York and many other cities, loudspeakers were set up to keep enthusiastic baseball fans informed of the progress of the game.

In the very first inning, Babe Ruth went to work to prove the experts wrong. He stepped into the batter's box and waited for the pitch. Facing him was the

Cardinals' work-horse pitcher and biggest winner, Wee Willie Sherdel. A stocky little left-hander, Sherdel was known as a "slow-ball artist." He tantalized the batters with curves and soft pitches. Many batters facing him were over-anxious and swung too soon, missing the ball by a mile.

But the Babe waited until he saw a pitch he liked. He brought his long bat around with a tremendous swing and—

Babe Ruth, unperturbed by Sherdel, is poised for a hit in the first game of the series.

crack!—he connected solidly. The ball shot into right center field, a long drive that bounced up against the wall. Ruth set off for first. As he rounded the base he hopped a few times to favor his knee, but he made it into second base easily.

The crowd roared its approval and kept up the shouting as stocky Lou Gehrig stepped to the plate.

Babe Ruth, on his way to first base after a long drive into right center field

He, too, waited for a good pitch and stepped into it with a powerful swing. The ball zoomed into right field for a solid base hit. Ruth raced for home and made it easily as Lou wound up at second.

The "Terrible Twins" had put the Yankees ahead, 1–0.

They stayed ahead, too. In the fourth, Ruth connected for another double. This time he got home easily, for long Bob Meusel whacked a home run, and the Babe just trotted in.

The game ended: Yankees, 4; Cardinals, 1.

Powerhouse Lou Gehrig, left, and the Babe were an unbeatable pair.

Cardinal fans were only a little downcast. " 'Old Pete' will stop 'em!" they insisted.

And the next day, pitching for the Cardinals, it *was* Old Pete—Grover Cleveland Alexander, hero of the 1926 Series victory over the Yanks. That year in his 16th season in the big leagues, Alexander still had a strong pitching arm and a marvelous ability to throw the ball right where he wanted it. In fact, he had beaten the Yanks twice in 1926 and saved the last game with brilliant relief pitching.

But 1928 was different. The Yankee "cripples" were all ready for him. In the very first inning one Yank got a single. Then Alexander's control deserted him and Babe Ruth got a base on balls. Up came Gehrig.

Old Pete pulled his cap down low on his forehead. He bounced the ball in his mitt a couple of times and glared at Lou.

"Well," he thought, "I used to get Lou out with a twister on the outside."

At the plate Lou watched Alexander carefully. He drew back his bat.

"If Alex gives me that outside screwball, I'm ready," he thought grimly.

Alexander glanced over his shoulder at the runners on the bases. He threw—right where he wanted it.

Gehrig was ready. He swung with all his might at the high, twisting pitch. And he connected. He hit a tremendous blow, mammoth, smashing, staggering, into the far right-field bleachers near the scoreboard. It was a home run, and the fans exploded with noise as a big "3" went up on the scoreboard for the Yankees.

The scrappy Cards rallied in the next inning. They tied the score when Lazzerri made a bad throw with his sore arm.

But then the Yanks' "Murderers' Row"

went to work and poured five more runs across. Old Pete was driven from the box. Final score: Yankees, 9; Cardinals, 3.

On the train to St. Louis for the next game, the Yankees were jubilant.

"Who said we were easy picking?" roared Babe Ruth.

Lou Gehrig walked down the aisle with a basket of fried chicken his mother had made.

"Let me at it," the Babe clamored.

"Hey, Babe, don't eat too much," cautioned the Yankee manager.

"Aw, Mom Gehrig's cooking never hurt anyone," said the Babe, tearing off a drumstick.

Perhaps Lou Gehrig picked up some extra strength from his mother's chicken. At any rate, the third game was Gehrig's game.

The Cardinals rallied in the second inning with three runs, this one by Jimmy Wilson.

Nearly 40,000 shouting St. Louisans packed Sportsman's Park to cheer their players. Big Jess Haines went to the mound to try to stop the Yanks with his fast-ball pitching. But once again the Yanks got revenge. Haines, too, had beaten them twice in 1926.

The Yanks gave the Cards a chance by letting in three runs on errors. But when they needed runs, Gehrig was there. In the second he whacked a towering home run that bounced on the bleacher roof and out into the street. Then in the fourth, with Ruth on first base, Lou powered a drive to deep center that rolled all the way to the wall. He raced around the bases for another home run. Later, his "Bustin' Twin" Ruth knocked in the last run of the game with a single, and the score was Yankees, 7; Cardinals, 3.

It rained the next day, and the players had the day off. As he often did, Babe Ruth stuck some baseballs in his pocket and headed for the hospital. He spent the afternoon laughing and joking with the sick children and handed out autographed baseballs.

One little boy with a broken leg called to him.

"I hate to see the Cardinals lose, but, but—could you hit a home run for me tomorrow?"

Ruth's big round face broke into a smile. "Why, I'll hit *two* for you!" he promised.

He did better than that. He hit three. For the second time in World Series play he did the impossible: he hit three home runs in one game.

The park was packed again. Wee Willie Sherdel went out to try his "slow stuff" on the Yankees again. Babe Ruth whacked one to the bleachers roof in the fourth, but the Cards still led, 2–1, when the seventh opened.

Then Ruth hit another one to the roof. Lou Gehrig came up next and hit an even longer home run toward the same spot. The "Terrible Twins" were wrecking the Cards again.

An inning later the Babe hit his third home run onto the roof. There was no stopping him. And his knee was no bother, for all he did was jog around the bases.

The "terrible twins," Ruth and Gehrig

The game ended: New York Yankees, 7; St. Louis Cardinals, 3. For the second year in a row the Yankees had won the world championship in four straight games.

"Pretty good for a bunch of cripples, eh?" said the grinning Babe.

Note: This was only the third crown for the Yankees, but there were many more to come. In 1962 they won their twentieth World Series. Some students of the game say, however, that the 1927–1928 Yankees were the greatest baseball team ever.

5 The Year of the Goose Egg

"The Giants can beat *any* American League team!"

That's the way the National League fans talked in October, 1905 about the New York Giants. Led by their fiery manager, John J. McGraw, the Giants had just won a close race for the National League championship.

The Philadelphia Athletics had won an even closer race for the American League title. These two teams would be the first to play in an organized World Series set up by baseball's National Commission.

Manager John J. McGraw, left, coaching a New York player at third

"Connie Mack's boys will murder those Giants!" was the cry of the American League fans. Tall and slender Cornelius McGillicuddy was known as Connie Mack. A clever manager, he had trained a team of exciting players. He had an unusually powerful pitching staff, but he had to finish the season without his star left-hander, Rube Waddell. The fun-loving Waddell had hurt his arm in a playful wrestling match and would not be able to pitch in the World Series.

Chunky John McGraw had brilliant pitchers, too, in Christy Mathewson and Joe McGinnity. "I'll use them every game if I can," he announced.

McGraw was a stern leader who drove his players to do their best. But he watched over them, too, as a shepherd watches his sheep. He was as shrewd a manager as anyone in baseball.

The first game was played in Philadelphia on Monday, October 9, when nearly 18,000 people crowded into a park built for 10,000. Spectators spilled out of the wooden stands and spread out all across deep center field. Outside the park twice as many clamored to get in.

Connie Mack sent out young Eddie Plank, his second-best left-hander, to pitch. Tall, silent Eddie was a tough competitor, who always gave his best.

The Giants came to bat in the first inning. The cheers were deafening when Plank set them down without a run. Up on the scoreboard went an "0" for the Giants, the first goose egg.

Young Christy Mathewson went out to the mound to pitch for the Giants. Mathewson and Plank had opposed each other many times in college games. Plank, pitching for Gettysburg College, had never beaten Mathewson, the star of the Bucknell College nine. Now Mathewson was determined to defeat his rival in the first big game of the first World Series.

Mathewson was tall and powerfully built. He had muscular shoulders and legs from playing football at Bucknell. For baseball, he had developed an amazing variety of pitches. Now he turned them all loose on the eager Athletics.

Zing! his fast ball popped into catcher Bresnahan's glove. The first Athletics batter swung hard and missed. Mathewson threw his curve and his knuckle ball. Then he threw his famous "fadeaway"—a ball that curved and dropped in the opposite direction from a regular curve ball. He always threw it when a batter least expected it. He had the Athletics hitting fast at slow balls, and slowly at fast balls. With marvelous control, he threw

76

Christy Mathewson

high, low, or in the middle when he pleased. When the Athletics did hit the ball, they usually couldn't hit it solidly and were easy outs.

The goose eggs continued to go up on the scoreboard for both sides, for three innings.

In the fourth inning, little Topsy Hartsel, an Athletics favorite, connected squarely with a Mathewson pitch for a single. Up on their feet jumped the Athletics fans, shouting for more.

Mathewson took off his cap. He ran his fingers through his tousled, curly hair. He set his jaw and pitched, harder than ever. Another goose egg went up for the Athletics.

Then the Giants came to bat again. Mathewson led off by banging one of Eddie Plank's pitches for a safe hit. As Mathewson raced for first, it was the turn

Climbing a tree outside the Polo Grounds was an inexpensive way to see the ball game!

of the Giant fans to roar. Before the inning was over the Giants had two more hits and a walk and a big "2" went up on the scoreboard. That was all Mathewson needed, although the Giants knocked in another run in the ninth. Final score: Giants, 3; Athletics, 0.

The next day, in New York, the Giant fans poured into the Polo Grounds stands,

"Chief" Bender, Philly's star pitcher, above, and the Giants' "Iron Man" Mc-Ginnity, left

sure of another triumph. The day was rather cold, but nearly 25,000 people fought their way through the gates. In deep center field, horse-drawn carriages lined up, full of eager spectators.

Connie Mack sent out Charles Albert Bender, his right-handed ace, to pitch. "Chief" Bender was a twenty-two-year-old Chippewa from Minnesota who had learned to pitch at Carlisle Indian School. He had a reputation for exhibiting top form when the competition was roughest. With a strong arm and a cool head, Bender pitched a game to match Mathewson's. The Giants were baffled by his clever delivery. They got only four hits, and not a run.

"Iron Man" Joe McGinnity pitched a stout game for the Giants. With his sweeping underhand delivery, Joe shot the ball across the plate at peculiar angles. At first, it looked as though he would blow the Athletics aside. But the usually strong Giant defense wobbled. Two errors played a big part in making the score Athletics, 3; Giants, 0.

It was an excited bunch of Athletics that got ready for the next day's game. They had tied the series. They were back home in Philadelphia. They didn't expect to meet Mathewson again until the fourth game.

Then it rained. The umpires called off Wednesday's game. Mathewson got another day's rest, and he was ready to pitch again on Thursday, October 12.

Once again Mathewson was invincible. He gave the Athletics only four hits—and no runs. Another long string of goose eggs went up on the scoreboard for the Athletics.

Connie Mack sent young Andy Coakley

to the mound. Only a year or two out of college, Andy had blossomed out with the best winning percentage in the American League for 1905. But he was no match for the rampaging Giants. They blasted out nine hits and, with the help of five Athletics errors, they brought the score to Giants, 9; Athletics, 0.

Now it was back to New York for the fourth game. Friday the thirteenth was bound to be unlucky for someone, and that someone turned out to be Eddie Plank. He went to the hill for the Athletics, and he pitched a fine game. Seven big goose eggs went up on the scoreboard for the Giants. Eddie gave them only four hits. But in the fourth inning, the Giants squeezed a run across the plate with no hits at all. Two Athletics errors did the trick.

One run was enough, for Joe McGinnity was in good form for the Giants. This time he was the winner, as he gave only five hits and blanked the Athletics all the way. Giants, 1; Athletics, 0.

The Giants needed only one more victory to take the World Series. Saturday's game could finish it off. A huge crowd packed the Polo Grounds. The Giants' pitcher— with only one day's rest—was Christy Mathewson.

For the Athletics, Connie Mack sent out his only winner, Chief Bender. What a battle it was!

The wiry Chief gave up only five hits to the Giants, but he gave up three bases on balls. Those bases were his downfall. In the fifth inning the Giants scored without a hit. Two walks and two sacrifices brought a run across. Then in the eighth,

"Chief" Bender pitched brilliantly, but he still couldn't measure up to Christy Mathewson.

Bender pitched to his rival Mathewson—and walked him! Mathewson raced home with the second and final run when Bresnahan whacked a long double.

The Athletics managed to get six hits off Mathewson. But every time they got a man on base, Mathewson pitched harder. Inning after inning went by. Up on the scoreboard went nothing but goose eggs for the Athletics. For the third time in six days, Mathewson shut out the champions of the American League. Score: New York Giants, 2; Philadelphia Athletics, 0.

In all the long history of the World Series since then, no one has equaled that record: pitching three complete shutout victories in one series. One reporter wrote, "The Athletics were simply 'bumfoozled' by Mathewson."

The Giants won the series, four games to one. Every game was a shutout, including

The 1905 Series was a disaster for Connie Mack and his Philadelphia Athletics.

the Athletics' one victory. That's still a record, too.

Connie Mack, the Athletics manager, said sadly, "I wish we'd had Waddell to pitch for us, too. But we have no excuse. We didn't make a run in four games."

John McGraw crowed, "Who said we were afraid of American Leaguers? We showed 'em the National's the only real big league!"

Giants fans, shouting and happy, poured out onto the playing field. They all wanted to shake hands with Christy Mathewson.

"You did it, boy! You gave 'em the goose egg!" they shouted.

Mathewson smiled broadly and tipped his cap. Then he ran for the dressing room. He could face the Athletics, but not that wild crowd.

Note: The Giants moved from New York in 1956, to become the San Francisco Giants.

The Athletics moved from Philadelphia to Kansas City in 1954, and then to Oakland, California in 1968.

6 Baseball Looks Ahead

The year 1968 was a big milestone for professional baseball—the hundredth year of its existence.

Rules have changed over these years, always with the hope of improving the great American game. Back in 1873 the rules makers found it necessary to prohibit fielders from catching flies in their hats! That brings a laugh today, but what would those rules makers say if they could see the huge gloves that baseball players use now?

Christy Mathewson's glove was tiny . . .

Those tough early baseballers played bare handed. The first fielder's glove didn't appear until 1883 and then it was pretty skimpy. Even since the World Series began, the change is startling. Look at the stubby glove on Christy Mathewson. Now study one of today's mitts—they look

. . . compared to today's baseball mitt.

as big as bushel baskets in comparison.
And they do tighten up the defense.

In the early days the pitcher had lots
of advantages. The ball was not very
lively. Sometimes the same ball was used
for a full game—or longer. If it got
scuffed or torn or dirty, it stayed in the

game just the same. If there was a tear in the cover, a pitcher could make the ball do some pretty funny tricks. And of course a dirty ball is harder for the batter to see. Nowadays umpires throw a ball out of the game for the tiniest mark on it. Sometimes dozens of balls are used in one game.

In 1910 the old-time "dead" ball was changed; the new official ball had a cork and rubber center. With this construction, a solidly hit ball traveled far and fast. Hitters could really whack it.

The whole strategy of the game began to change with the lively ball. In the old days John McGraw had perfected the "hit-and-run" game. He taught his batters to place their hits away from the opposing fielders. The cry was "hit 'em where they ain't!", and the Giants were experts. They even used a bat with a flat surface for

making clever bunts, but that was too un-
fair, and the rules were changed to call for
round bats.

When the sluggers, like Babe Ruth and
Lou Gehrig, began pounding out doubles
and triples and home runs, the pitchers
were in trouble. To be effective many had
to develop a wide variety of pitches, like
the "slider" and "fork-ball" and "screwball." Teams had more pitchers, too, so
that relief pitchers could be rushed in at
any minute. This is a far cry from the
days when "Iron Man" Joe McGinnity
used to pitch both games of a double-
header!

To "shake-up" the sluggers a little,
pitchers even began to pitch as close as
possible to a dangerous batter. Many a
howl of rage went up from startled batters when the ball came too close. Many
a pitcher was accused of deliberately

Baseball players today wearing helmets

throwing a "beanball" when he insisted
he was only "brushing the batter back."
So many batters *were* hit and injured that
teams began to require every batter to
wear a protective helmet.

A favorite trick of some pitchers was
the "spitball." When a baseball has a lot
of moisture on one side, a pitcher can
make it do a real "dipsy-doodle" as it

crosses the plate. In 1920 a rule was passed against "doctoring" the ball in any way. But some pitchers secretly continued. Managers would rush out to the umpire: "Let me see that ball! That was a spitter!" But if it had been, the catcher had wiped it clean. How could anyone prove it?

After the 1968 season the leagues resolved to enforce the new rule preventing a pitcher from touching his mouth before a pitch. For 1968 was known as "The Year of the Pitcher." Batting had slumped to new lows. In the American League it looked as though the champion batter would have a percentage *under* .300 for the first time in history. In the closing days of the season Carl Yastrzemski just managed to push his winning average to .301.

To help the batters even more, the pitcher's mound was lowered from fifteen inches high to ten inches high for 1969. Even tougher for the pitcher, the strike zone was made smaller.

As styles of playing change, rules will continue to change to keep the game fair to offense and defense, to speed up the game, and to keep it interesting.

But it isn't the rules that make the game exciting, it is the players themselves, who develop their skills to a high degree no matter what the rules. Brilliant new players are fighting their way up, determined to outdo the great pitchers like Lolich and Gibson and the explosive hitters like Kaline and Brock.

So World Series time each year promises even more thrills as professional baseball rolls along in its second century.